American Symbols

The Star-Spangled Banner

by Debbie L. Yanuck

Consultant:
Melodie Andrews, Ph.D.
Associate Professor of Early American History
Minnesota State University, Mankato

Capstone
press

Mankato, Minnesota

Capstone Press
151 Good Counsel Drive, P.O. Box 669, Mankato, Minnesota 56002
http://www.capstone-press.com

Library of Congress Cataloging-in-Publication Data
Yanuck, Debbie L.
     The star-spangled banner / by Debbie L. Yanuck.
     p. cm.—(American symbols)
     Summary: Briefly discusses the authorship of the poem later set to music that became the national anthem of the United States as well as the flag itself.
     Includes bibliographical references (p. 24) and index.
     ISBN 0-7368-2293-3 (hardcover)
     1. Baltimore, Battle of, Baltimore, Md., 1814—Juvenile literature. 2. United States—History—War of 1812—Flags—Juvenile literature. 3. Flags—United States—History—19th century—Juvenile literature. 4. Key, Francis Scott, 1779–1843—Juvenile literature. 5. Star-spangled banner (Song)—Juvenile literature. [1. Star-spangled banner (Song) 2. Flags.] I. Title. II. Series
E356 .B2Y36 2004
782.42'1599'0973—dc21   2002156488

Editorial Credits
Roberta Schmidt, editor; Linda Clavel, designer; Kelly Garvin, photo researcher;
     Eric Kudalis and Karen Risch, product planning editors

Photo Credits
Copyright 2002. Frank J. Hackinson Publishing Co. All Rights Reserved. Used by
     Permission., 13
Corbis/Steve Chenn, cover; Richard Hutchings, 5; Mug Shots, 7; Bettmann, 15
Getty Images/Diane Sobolewski, 19
Library of Congress, 11, 17, 20, 21
North Wind Picture Archives, 9, 12

1 2 3 4 5 6 08 07 06 05 04 03

Table of Contents

Star-Spangled Banner Fast Facts

- "The Star-Spangled Banner" is a symbol of courage and respect.

- Francis Scott Key wrote "The Star-Spangled Banner" in 1814.

- "The Star-Spangled Banner" started as a poem called "The Defense of Fort McHenry." The poem is sung to the English tune "To Anacreon in Heaven."

- "The Star-Spangled Banner" has four verses, but most people know only the first verse.

- In 1813, Mary Pickersgill and her daughter Caroline made the flag that Francis Scott Key saw. It is 42 feet (13 meters) long and 30 feet (9 meters) high and weighs 200 pounds (91 kilograms).

- "The Star-Spangled Banner" became the national anthem of the United States on March 3, 1931.

NO
Aa Bb Cc Dd Ee Ff Gg Hh
The ABC Song
a b c d e f g
h i j k
l m n o p
q r s
t u v
w x y z
Now I know my abc's.
next time won't you sing with me?

Symbol of Courage and Respect

The song "The Star-Spangled Banner" is a symbol of courage and respect. Americans showed courage at the time the song was written. Today, Americans play and sing "The Star-Spangled Banner" to show respect for the United States.

spangled
covered with decorations

Francis Scott Key

Francis Scott Key wrote "The Star-Spangled Banner" in 1814. During the War of 1812 (1812–1814), Key went to a British ship near Baltimore, Maryland. Key went there to help a friend. His friend was a prisoner on the ship.

prisoner
a person who is held by force

9

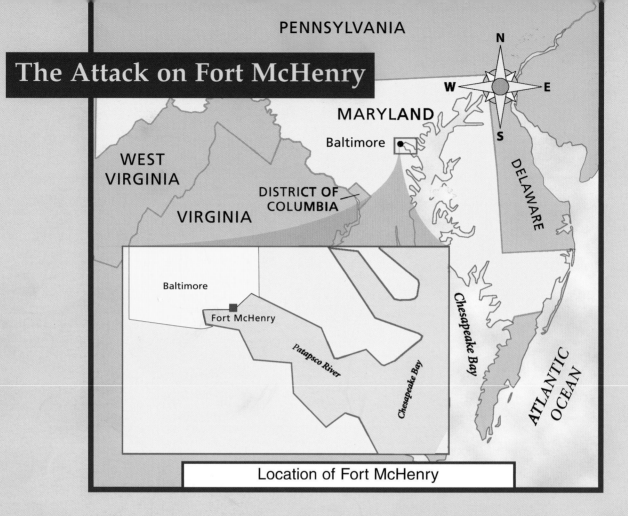

Location of Fort McHenry

The British attacked Fort McHenry on September 13, 1814. Key was kept on the British ship during the attack. The British and Americans fought all day and night.

10

Key looked toward the fort the next
morning. Through the smoke, he saw
the U.S. flag flying over the fort. He then
knew the Americans had won the battle.

A Poem Becomes a Song

After the battle, Key wrote a poem about the fight and the flag. He called his poem "The Defense of Fort McHenry." A Baltimore newspaper printed the poem.

The Star-spangled banner.

O say! can you see by the dawn's early light
What so proudly we hail'd at the twilight's last gleaming
Whose broad stripes and bright stars, through the clouds of the fight,
O'er the ramparts we watch'd were so gallantly streaming?
And the rocket's red glare — the bomb bursting in air
Gave proof through the night that our flag was still there?
O say, does that star-spangled banner yet wave
O'er the land of the free & the home of the brave? —

Later, people added music to the poem.

The song became known as "The

Star-Spangled Banner."

The Other Star-Spangled Banner

The flag that flew at Fort McHenry in 1814 is also called the Star-Spangled Banner. From 1874 until 1907, it hung in the Boston Navy Yard. Today, the flag can be seen at the Smithsonian Institution in Washington, D.C.

anthem
a national song

The National Anthem

"The Star-Spangled Banner" became popular in the late 1800s. The U.S. military sang the song when they raised and lowered the flag. In 1931, Congress made "The Star-Spangled Banner" the national anthem of the United States.

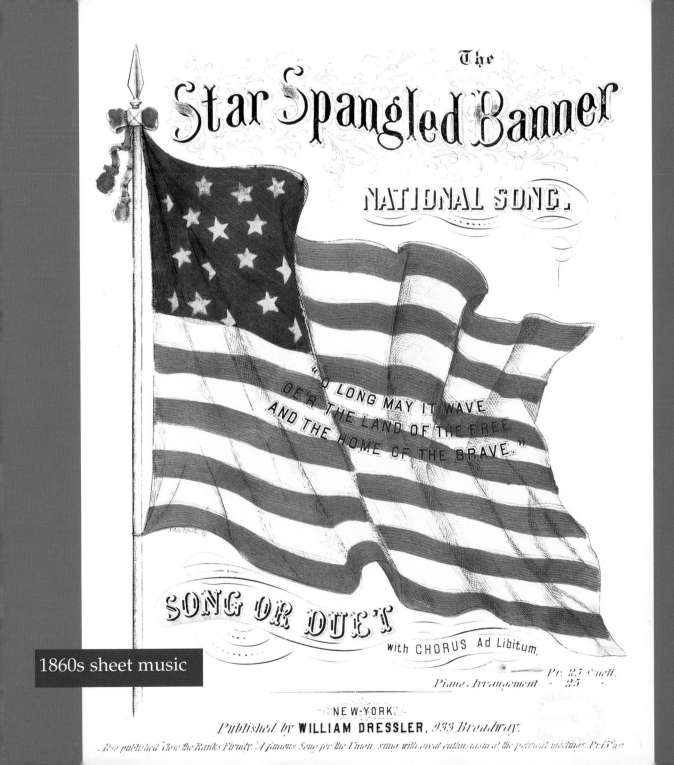

1860s sheet music

17

The Star-Spangled Banner Today

Today, Americans sing and play "The Star-Spangled Banner" at many events. They sing it before most sporting events. They also play it for military occasions. Americans show respect for the United States when they sing and play "The Star-Spangled Banner."

Timeline

1813—Mary Pickersgill and her daughter Caroline sew a large flag for Fort McHenry.

1814—Francis Scott Key writes a poem about the battle and the U.S. flag.

1814—The British attack Fort McHenry.

1895—The U.S. Army and Navy start singing "The Star-Spangled Banner."

1931—"The Star-Spangled Banner" becomes the national anthem of the United States.

1916—President WoodrowWilson orders "The Star-Spangled Banner" to be played at all military events.

Hands On: Write a Poem

Francis Scott Key wrote "The Star-Spangled Banner" as a poem. You can write your own poem about the United States.

What You Need

Paper
Pencil
Crayons

What You Do

1. Think about words and symbols important to the United States. Ask friends and family what words they think best describe the United States.
2. Write about your ideas and feelings for the United States. Some poems use words that rhyme. Your poem does not have to rhyme.
3. After you write your poem, use crayons to decorate your paper.
4. Read or sing your poem to your friends and family.

Words to Know

anthem (AN-thuhm)—a national song

battle (BAT-uhl)—a fight between two armies

national (NASH-uh-nuhl)—to do with or belonging to a country as a whole

occasion (uh-KAY-zhuhn)—a special or important event

popular (POP-yuh-lur)—liked or enjoyed by many people

prisoner (PRIZ-uhn-ur)—a person who is held by force

symbol (SIM-buhl)—an object that stands for something else

Read More

Gregson, Susan R. *Francis Scott Key: Patriotic Poet.* Let Freedom Ring. Mankato, Minn.: Bridgestone Books, 2003.

Quiri, Patricia Ryon. *The National Anthem.* A True Book. New York: Children's Press, 1998.

Internet Sites

Do you want to find out more about "The Star-Spangled Banner"? Let FactHound, our fact-finding hound dog, do the research for you.

Here's how:
1) Visit *http://www.facthound.com*
2) Type in the **Book ID** number:
    0736822933
3) Click on **FETCH IT**.

FactHound will fetch Internet sites picked by our editors just for you.

Index